Leanne
SPENCER

SUSTAIN

Mastering the
high-performance
paradox

R^ethink

First published in Great Britain in 2025
by Rethink Press (www.rethinkpress.com)

© Copyright Leanne Spencer

All rights reserved. No part of this publication may be reproduced, stored in or introduced into a retrieval system, or transmitted, in any form, or by any means (electronic, mechanical, photocopying, recording or otherwise) without the prior written permission of the publisher.

The right of Leanne Spencer to be identified as the author of this work has been asserted by her in accordance with the Copyright, Designs and Patents Act 1988.

This book is sold subject to the condition that it shall not, by way of trade or otherwise, be lent, resold, hired out, or otherwise circulated without the publisher's prior consent in any form of binding or cover other than that in which it is published and without a similar condition including this condition being imposed on the subsequent purchaser.

Disclaimer: The use of any information in this book, including any suggested nutrition or exercise, is solely at the reader's own risk. You should always seek medical advice before undertaking any diet or exercise or starting an exercise programme. Neither Rethink Press nor the author can be held liable or responsible in respect of any and all injuries, losses, damages, expense, or other adverse effects incurred while undertaking any of the exercise or other activities described in this book.

Illustrations by Shane Barrell

For Rourke and Raven

Contents

Introduction		**1**
1	**My Story**	**5**
	Sustaining resilience	11
2	**Why Sustain And Why Now?**	**15**
	The impact of AI	16
	Burnout is on the rise	17
	Modern workplace culture	18
	Political, economic and climate pressures	19
	The Hans Rosling paradox	20
3	**The Paradox Of Wellbeing And High Performance**	**23**
	What is a paradox?	26
	The paradox mindset	28

4	**The Sustain Framework**	**31**
	Acknowledging the science	34
5	**Values Build Boundaries**	**37**
	Getting clear on your personal values	41
	The paradox of values and boundaries	45
6	**Identity Inspires Ownership**	**47**
	Adapt and stay in the game	50
	Identity isn't about labels	52
	The paradox of identity and behaviour	53
7	**Community Creates Connection**	**57**
	Social connection improves stress resilience	60
	The Blue Zones	61
	Seeking new connections	63
	The paradox of community and connection	65
8	**Resources Support Resilience**	**67**
	The Minimal Effective Day	72
	Rocks and pebbles	73

The paradox of resources and resilience	75
A Final Message: The Ultimate Paradox	**79**
Bibliography	**83**
Bonus Resources	**89**
The Author	**93**

Introduction

What if the real key to high performance isn't how hard you push yourself but how effectively you're able to sustain your energy, mood and motivation?

This book is for anyone who has wondered how to maintain good health and wellbeing without slowing down or suffering from chronic stress or burnout. It can be challenging to manage the tension between delivering results and preserving your energy, leading you to feel as though you're caught in a paradox.

Sustain will show you how to resolve that tension and cultivate a paradox mindset. It's about building habits that support your resilience and optimise your energy, mood and motivation – because *everything* is downstream of energy, mood and motivation. This book is a deep dive into resilience viewed from a novel perspective. It's for anyone who wants to perform at a high level without trading tomorrow's wellbeing for today's success.

You'll learn how to:

- Use your values to make better decisions under pressure
- Anchor your identity to take ownership of habits and behaviours
- Strengthen your community to boost stress resilience and mental health
- Build daily non-negotiables to sustain your energy, mood and motivation

The goal is to develop the tools to thrive in life and help solve the challenges of work (product

INTRODUCTION

innovation, sales or growth) while also having the resilience required to make a meaningful impact on the world's problems. All of this can be achieved without breaking yourself in the process. That's what it means to *sustain*. This book will show you how.

ONE
My Story

I sometimes think of my life in two halves: everything that happened before March 2012, and everything that has happened since. I was not in a good place in 2012, or for the previous couple of years. I was working as an account director in a sales role, but I was tired, emotionally drained and, frankly, burnt out. I was struggling with the demands of my job and the lack of enthusiasm I had for City life. I felt I wasn't being true to who I am, doing a role I didn't care about in an environment that wasn't for me. I wasn't dressing the way I wanted to or behaving as I knew I should, and I was medicating this lack of authenticity with alcohol (a lot of it). My personal values were not aligned with who I wanted to be, and I had no sense of identity, of what I stood for.

And then came that fateful March.

I went into a sales meeting hoping to close a large order, but within a few minutes of the meeting beginning, to my dismay and disappointment, the client informed me that the deal was off. Despondent, I headed home to seriously reevaluate my options. After a short but intense period of reflection, I decided that a big change was needed, and that same weekend I resigned from my job in a move that appeared abrupt to many around me, but which had been bubbling under the surface for a while.

After a few weeks of rest and recovery, I needed to get back to some form of work. It was clear to me that my next move needed to be something focused on health and wellbeing, and that I could move into with relatively little training. I've always loved sport and fitness, and so I signed on to do a Diploma in Personal Training, qualifying that summer. I thoroughly enjoyed the course and I won my first client by placing an ad in a local internet forum. I couldn't believe that my new job was to meet clients in a local park and look after their fitness goals. I thought I'd hit the jackpot. I didn't yet look much like a personal trainer, but I bought a few bits of kit, including a kettlebell, medicine ball and some boxing pads, and set off to meet my client. I'd sold my car by this point, so I was cycling around with all that kit in a holdall that I wore across my back. If it was wet or there were a lot of leaves on the ground, I'd skid off the bike, so I quickly upgraded to a decent rucksack.

From these humble beginnings I grew the business to six figures and had a number of personal trainers working for me.

All our sessions were delivered in local parks, as a key part of our offering was getting clients outside in nature and natural light, no matter what the time or the weather. We had great feedback, high renewal and retention rates, and we generally felt good about what we were doing. There was just one thing, which came up during a team meeting at which everyone seemed a bit flat. We all knew we were excellent personal trainers. We were well-qualified, continually improving our skills and developing our knowledge through books and courses, and we were motivated, personable and empathetic. However, we all felt as though we weren't delivering the best outcome for our clients despite our good intentions. Clients were arriving to us tired and stressed and, frankly, what they actually needed was to take their rucksacks off their backs (literally and metaphorically) and go for a walk, not force themselves through a high-intensity interval session. We felt we could do a much better job if we looked at health from a holistic standpoint, and helped our clients understand that what they *thought* they needed was possibly the last thing they should be doing. To do that, though, we needed to help them overcome the paradox of physical fitness: often, the gains we expect come from rest or reduced intensity, not working harder or training faster. Instead of prescribing more intensity, we began to explore what a broader, intelligent training programme could look like.

Physical fitness is an important part of wellbeing, but we all agreed it's just one component. We therefore devised a holistic representation of wellbeing and called it the Six Signals – sleep, mental health, energy, body composition, digestive health and fitness. We created coaching and bespoke personal training packages that were based on sophisticated tests and cutting-edge science, including DNA testing, blood testing for various biomarkers and stool testing for gut health. We used data from wearable technology devices such as the Whoop Band and the Oura Ring, which provided insights into our clients' sleep, activity and recovery metrics, eliminating guesswork. We had at our disposal a wealth of data about each of our clients and were able to create highly personalised personal training programmes for them.

What we found, however, surprised us: the more data we had about a client, the more overwhelmed they felt, which affected their progress. It was another paradox. We realised that resilience isn't about fitness, or data or test results; those elements can be helpful, but what contributes to lasting resilience is the strength of the foundation upon which you build consistent habits. We need energy, mood and motivation to thrive in life, be open to opportunity and overcome our own personal challenges. For those of us who work, we need these three factors to help the organisations we work for to overcome challenges, whether that's in sales, product development, innovation or growth. More broadly, we also need energy, mood and motivation to meaningfully contribute to solving the world's problems.

Sustaining resilience

When finding or developing resilience, the question is, of course, how? We don't lack information. In fact, that's part of the problem. There's an overwhelming amount of information available to us. The challenge is filtering this information to find out what's relevant and trustworthy and then applying it to our own set of circumstances. It's about building habits that support our energy, mood and motivation, because everything else lies downstream of these three key elements. It's about ensuring we can *sustain* ourselves through life.

I began to think more deeply about how we can embed lasting habits. I wanted to take a deep dive into what resilience is and how we can develop it. I looked for a fresh approach, and that's how the Sustain Framework came to be. The Sustain Framework is comprised of four pillars:

SUSTAIN

1. A strong sense of personal **values**
2. A clear sense of your **identity**
3. A close **community** of people in your network
4. **Resources** that support resilience

That's what this book is all about.

Once I'd developed this framework, the next step was to find a way to convey these ideas to many people at once, not one at a time. This was the only way we'd make a significant impact. Things really changed for me in 2016 when I had a meeting with my first boss, Julian, a straight-talking Northerner who taught me a huge amount about business and the art of selling. I explained to him our philosophies around personalised fitness and that we had important messages to share. The limiting factor was, of course, that within our model we could only deliver it one person at a time. My conversation with Julian encouraged me to think about sharing my message at scale, through public speaking. I'd done a lot of presenting to small groups in my sales roles, but not public speaking to larger audiences.

My team did some research and discovered that Wandsworth TEDx were looking for speakers, and the theme was *'Perspective' which aims to challenge the prevailing orthodoxy* – perfect for the idea I had in mind. My idea was to refocus people away from the aesthetic benefits of fitness to the functional and longevity benefits of being healthy. I wanted to draw attention to what we can do with our bodies rather than what they look like. The talk was called 'Why fitness is more important than weight', and as of the time of writing, has over 132,000 views (Spencer, 2016). Writing and researching the talk, then delivering it live to over 100 people, made me realise that I love the art of public speaking and wanted to make this my profession.

Starting with small groups of ten to fifty people, I began to craft talks that addressed big topics like stress management, resilience and burnout prevention, but with humour, lightness and ease. Stories are what resonate with people. You can see the energy and focus of a group change when you tell them a story versus informing them about tips or educating them on facts. I developed and worked on my stagecraft until I felt confident that I was able to have a real impact on my audience in an entertaining and engaging way.

I am now one of the UK's leading speakers on wellbeing, resilience and high performance, and I've spoken to tens of thousands of people virtually and in person. My mission is to motivate and inspire people to take ownership of their wellbeing and ensure they have the energy, mood and motivation to thrive in life. I hope this book does that for you.

TWO
Why Sustain And Why Now?

The world is changing at an unprecedented pace, with climate change, economic instability and technological disruption reshaping how we live and work. A recent study of 2,000 people (including 590 employers) commissioned by outdoor education provider Inspiring Learning, revealed that a soft-skills gap is having a negative impact on UK workplaces (Moss, 2024). The research showed that the biggest gap in soft skills was among people aged 18 to

25. Employers noted that 37% of their Gen Z employees lacked communication skills, 27% were deficient in problem-solving and 28% lacked resilience.

The impact of AI

In 2023, Sam Altman was asked what he thought the critical skills would be for kids growing up who wanted to code, given that AI is now able to do much of it already. He replied, 'Number one, you need to be very resilient' (Merani, 2023). We've already experienced a lot of change through the implementation of AI, and it's likely to have a significant impact on our lives and the types of jobs available to future generations. Developing soft skills, like resilience and adaptability to change, will be as critical as learning a traditional trade or developing a specific area of expertise. This is especially important because of the pace of change that AI is ushering in.

Burnout is on the rise

A survey of 4,418 UK adults conducted by YouGov found that, last year, one in three (34%) adults experienced high or extreme levels of pressure or stress 'always' or 'often', compared with 35% the previous year (Mental Health UK, 2025). Burnout is on the rise, and yet, according to our research from over 246 participating organisations (Spencer, 2025), many organisations still lack a formal wellbeing strategy. Paradoxically, 72% reported burnout incidents in the past year, yet 54% of organisations said they have no structured approach to address it. Nearly half of the employees featured in our research reported difficulties managing stress, recovery and work-life balance. A study by Ciphr (2024) found that the average UK adult feels stressed 10.3 days per month, with one in nine experiencing stress on a daily basis. This presents an ongoing challenge to our resilience.

Modern workplace culture

Another aggravating factor is workplace culture, with 34% of employees describing their meeting culture as intense, contributing to exhaustion and disengagement (Spencer, 2025). A major factor driving burnout is the erosion of workplace relationships. Hybrid and remote working have reshaped our professional interactions, and while they offer flexibility, they also contribute to disconnection. Our research shows that 75% of employees working remotely or in hybrid roles report weaker social ties and smaller networks. Paradoxically, technology has made connection easier than ever, yet people appear to feel more isolated.

For those of us who work in organisations, resilience is required to navigate the challenges of stakeholder management, fundraising, sales, growth and innovation. Creativity, commitment and collaboration are impossible without a foundation of resilience. Most of us want longevity in our careers, but that requires sustaining energy, mood and motivation over the long term.

Political, economic and climate pressures

With everything that's going on in our interconnected world, it can be easy to feel overwhelmed. News outlets are on a 24/7 cycle, headlines can be seen on dynamic advertising screens, in social media feeds and pop-ups, and it can feel as though there's no escape from negativity. All these factors can challenge our resilience and our ability to maintain a positive mindset. While things are bad in the world, and it's definitely a period of intense change, it is important to recognise that things can be bad but also getting better. A key element of resilience is the ability to hold those two opposing thoughts in your mind at the same time. This is called a paradox mindset.

The Hans Rosling paradox

In their excellent book *Factfulness*, Hans Rosling, along with Ola Rosling and Anna Rosling Rönnlund (Rosling et al, 2018), posit that things are bad in the world, but they are also improving in ways many of us don't realise. Rosling suggests we have to overcome our 'dramatic instincts' which can lead us to view the world in a distorted way and negatively affect our resilience.

For example, when asked how many girls finish primary school in all the low-income countries across the world, most people answered 20% (the correct answer is 60%). When asked what has happened to the population of the world living in extreme poverty in the last twenty years, most people thought it had doubled. It had in fact halved. When asked how the number of deaths caused by natural disasters had changed over the last 100 years, most people thought it had doubled, whereas in fact it too has halved.

You can take the Factfulness Quiz by visiting https://factfulnessquiz.com.

Rosling is illustrating that it's easy to fall into the trap of thinking that things are bad. It is true that bad things happen every day and the world certainly has its challenges, but we need to reconcile this with the fact that it is also getting better. It's also true that we need resilience to be able to hold these two ideas in our minds at the same time. This particularly applies to wellbeing and resilience.

Let's explore why.

THREE

The Paradox Of Wellbeing And High Performance

I met someone recently who shared a cautionary tale about the misconceptions we often have about resilience and high performance. Joe worked for a fast-paced tech startup in a role he loved, and he was fully committed to the company's purpose and direction it was heading in. When he signed up to join the team, he was told the hours would sometimes be long, and sometimes it would be 'all hands to the pump', but this was the type of work he wanted to do and the type of environment he was used to.

The hours were often long, and Joe found himself feeling tired and under-energised. He would sleep in at the weekends but couldn't catch up. The sleep debt grew, and he became permanently tired, fuelling himself on coffee and energy drinks. He started to develop headaches, which he could medicate with painkillers and drinking more water, but this only temporarily lessened the pain. The headaches progressed until they became a strange sensation in his face and a tightening of the facial muscles, which he found uncomfortable and disturbing. However, Joe continued to ignore the signs and maintained his frenetic pace of work.

One afternoon, a sales rep asked Joe to join him the following day at a client meeting which was to take place 150 miles away and necessitated an early start. Joe agreed, but when he woke, he didn't feel good at all. The tightness in his facial muscles had worsened and he felt tired

WELLBEING AND HIGH PERFORMANCE

and anxious. Cancelling the meeting wasn't up to him and he didn't feel he could let the sales rep down, so Joe set off down the motorway, all the while feeling progressively worse. He had to stop off at several points to compose himself, but by the time he arrived at the client, something deeply worrying had happened. The entire left side of his face had drooped and was paralysed. It was later diagnosed as Bell's Palsy, and he was unable to work for several weeks while he recovered. Joe now has a different perspective on the role of wellbeing within a fast-paced business culture.

It's quite extreme to develop Bell's Palsy, but you may recognise elements of this story in yourself. We quite often sacrifice wellbeing for workload, and I accept that sometimes, in the short term, that might be necessary. The paradox here is that Joe believed relentless effort and long hours were the key to high performance, but they led to his breakdown rather than to his success. High performance isn't about working harder at all costs but working sustainably. The very thing Joe sacrificed, his wellbeing, was the foundation of what he was trying to achieve.

What is a paradox?

A paradox exists when two seemingly contradictory things are true at the same time. Put another way, a paradox is a self-contradictory statement or scenario that challenges conventional thinking. A somewhat glib example of a paradox is the supermarket self-checkout. In theory, it's designed to save time, but you often end up calling for assistance, dealing with errors and feeling more frustrated than if you'd just queued for a cashier. What was meant to be efficient becomes a bottleneck. Have you ever found yourself caught in a situation where you've sent a text message to someone that bears no resemblance to what you thought you'd typed? That pesky autocorrect has taken your words and turned them into a message

WELLBEING AND HIGH PERFORMANCE

that's cryptic or downright inappropriate! That's the paradox of time-saving technology.

There are plenty of examples of paradoxes in everyday life, and if you're curious about them there are several museums in London dedicated to paradoxes (including the Paradox Museum and the Twist Museum).

Here are three further examples of the paradox of wellbeing and high performance:

1. **The Rest Versus Results Paradox:** If you never take a break, there's a good chance that your body will break you. Elite athletes don't just train hard, they proactively focus on recovery, understanding that no one can perform at the highest levels all year round. We need to see ourselves as business athletes and prioritise rest as well as effort.

2. **The Hustle Versus Stagnation Paradox:** Working nonstop feels productive, but it's often the fastest route to burnout and bad

decisions. Some of the most successful people swear that, by doing less (taking breaks, blocking off thinking time, even scheduling downtime to spark creativity), they are more productive. Slowing down helps you speed up.

3. **The Selfish Versus Selfless Paradox:** Taking time for yourself and prioritising healthy habits such as regular exercise, hobbies or downtime can sometimes feel decadent or even might seem selfish. But when you're healthier, happier and recharged, you have more to give. The people who take care of themselves aren't just better for themselves; they're better for everyone around them.

The paradox mindset

A paradox mindset is the ability to embrace and navigate seemingly contradictory ideas or concepts without feeling the need to choose

WELLBEING AND HIGH PERFORMANCE

one over the other, just as Hans Rosling and his collaborators suggested. Instead of seeing things in either/or terms (eg, wellbeing or high performance), a paradox mindset sees them as both/and (wellbeing fuels high performance). Some might say it's a Jedi mind trick, but you'll probably find instances where you already apply this mindset even if you aren't consciously aware of it.

If we want to maintain our resilience, we need to face into this paradox and be comfortable holding two ideas in our heads at the same time. Wellbeing and high performance are mutually inclusive. People with a paradox mindset recognise that tensions aren't problems to be solved but dynamics to be managed. They resist binary thinking and instead look for ways to integrate competing demands in a way that enhances both.

The Sustain Framework requires us to adopt a paradox mindset and consider resilience in a novel way, based on a strong sense of values, identity, community and resources.

FOUR
The Sustain Framework

Beyond our work, one of our greatest purposes as human beings is to contribute, to experience life fully, and to make the most of our opportunities. True resilience allows us to do that.

The Sustain Framework is about reinforcing your resilience with a strong set of values upon which you can build boundaries around your habits and behaviours, keeping you on the right path. It's about having a strong sense of identity; being clear about the type of person you are and the code you live by. It's about having a solid community around you, because community creates connections. Finally, it's about having resources that support resilience, the daily non-negotiables that keep you well.

There are four key principles in the Sustain Framework:

1. **Values build boundaries.** What's important to you and what's the code you live by? What we value most gets prioritised, and our values are the foundations upon which our habits are built, and around which we can set our boundaries. Having strong values creates the energy and motivation to overcome barriers to change and develop consistent habits, which has a huge impact on our resilience.

2. **Identity inspires ownership.** Who do you want to be and what do you want

THE SUSTAIN FRAMEWORK

your impact in the world to be? A positive sense of identity can help you feel good about yourself and can be a source of strength and motivation when faced with adversity. Identity is who you are when things get tough.

3. **Community creates connection.** Community is about being connected to the people around you. Within communities, trust can grow and flourish, which drives productivity and improves collaboration, contributes to increasing psychological safety and promotes authenticity.

4. **Resources support resilience.** The resources that will build and support your resilience are the habits and routines that keep you healthy and mentally robust, or, put another way, they are the toolkit that supports good wellbeing for everyone. These habits might include mental health techniques, good sleep practices,

energy and mood boosting activities and physical exercise. They are the daily non-negotiables that keep you well, a result of small changes that have a big impact over time.

When we prioritise these four principles, we're better positioned to:

- Overcome barriers to change by connecting to values and identity
- Overcome the sense of guilt many people have about prioritising wellbeing
- Learn to deal with the fast pace of change that has become the new normal
- Develop the tools and mindset required to thrive in a high-performance culture

Acknowledging the science

There are a number of robust scientific studies that link values to resilience. According to a study by Sheldon and Elliot (1999), when your life aligns with your values, you feel more in control. In other words, you have more autonomy, which is a key part of motivation in Self-Determination Theory.

There's also evidence that reflecting on your values, a practice known as self-affirmation, lowers cortisol and sharpens problem-solving abilities when under stress. That means you perform better *and* stay calmer (Creswell et al, 2005).

Now more than ever, we need our resilience, and that's what the Sustain Framework is here to give us. Let's get stuck in!

FIVE
Values Build Boundaries

Simone Biles is one of the most decorated gymnasts in the world, winning eleven Olympic medals and thirty World Championships. She made history as the first African American to win the all-around title, a groundbreaking achievement that showcased her extraordinary talent. At the Tokyo Olympics, Biles made a decision that redefined what it means to be a champion, not by winning medals, but by staying true to her values.

SUSTAIN

The timing of the Tokyo Olympics probably felt strange for the athletes. Originally scheduled for 2020, the one-year postponement disrupted carefully planned training cycles, peaking strategies and mental preparation. Strict COVID-19 restrictions meant competing in empty arenas, without any of the usual energy and atmosphere that most athletes thrive on. Many faced disrupted training, limited access to facilities and cancelled qualification events, making preparing for the Olympics an unpredictable and discombobulating experience. The uncertainty of whether the games would even take place must have added an extra layer of mental and emotional strain. Additionally, Olympians are conditioned to peak every four years, and the unexpected fifth year will have had a significant impact on them, especially for those nearing retirement.

Only those close to her will know how Biles was feeling when she got off the plane in Tokyo, but as far as anyone outside of her close circle was concerned, it was business as usual. The world was expecting to see another standout performance, and a podium finish. Biles' sport is comprised of four disciplines. First up is the vault, then the balance beam, the uneven bars and finally the floor exercises. Here's what happened in Tokyo on 27 July 2021, as millions watched on television. We saw the familiar sight of the world's leading gymnast approach the vault and go through her pre-routine ritual. Looking down the twenty-five metres of runway, we watched as she took a deep breath and rubbed the chalk into her hands. Biles positioned her toes behind the white line, and took another deep breath, before accelerating towards the springboard. All seemed well until she hit the springboard and landed on the vault. Immediately, we could tell something was very wrong. She had attempted a difficult move called the Anamar Vault, which includes a 2.5-twist in the air, however, mid-air, she lost spatial awareness and only completed 1.5 twists before landing awkwardly. She quickly left the floor looking very upset.

SUSTAIN

What Biles experienced was a phenomenon called the Twisties. The Twisties is a dangerous mental block that disrupts spatial awareness, or proprioception, which is your sense of where your body is in space. Realising the danger this posed, she chose to withdraw from the rest of her events, stating she was prioritising her wellbeing, integrity and self-respect over external expectations. In a high-performance culture that often glorifies pushing through at all costs, Biles prioritised her own values over the demands of others. Despite the pressure she would have faced from her team as well as the world's media, Biles stayed true to her values to protect both her mental and physical health. There is a powerful lesson here for us all when it comes to setting boundaries around our wellbeing.

Getting clear on your personal values

Elon Musk has suggested we should strive to be a multiplanetary species, but I want us to be a multispecies planet first. One of my most important values is symbiotic living. I want to live symbiotically with nature and animals. We do not generally treat animals well and we are not taking care of our planet. These arguments are for another book, but living symbiotically is an important value for me. It informs my decisions about what I eat, the purchases I make and the places I visit. For example, I became vegetarian in 2022 (for animal welfare reasons), but I missed eating meat and certainly missed the variety that meat-eaters have in pubs and restaurants. The vegetarian options aren't always great when travelling, and I was sometimes tempted by a ham and cheese sandwich (an old favourite when I was a meat eater). What kept me from succumbing to that temptation was reconnecting to my value of symbiotic living (and animal welfare). The value created the boundary, and all I needed to do was respect that boundary.

Another value of mine is being energetic and having a dynamic approach to life. If I want to have good energy, I know there are certain boundaries I need to maintain around my work/life balance and the time I allocate to my health and fitness. I'll ringfence my exercise sessions and protect that time as though it was an appointment with a client. I ensure I have an eight-hour sleep window wherever possible so that I can get at least seven hours of sleep. I prioritise movement throughout the day, and I prioritise healthy eating and hydration. I'm not pretending that I'm perfect in all regards, but I value being energetic and dynamic above the temptations of dopaminergic foods and lots of Netflix, and it's those values that build my boundaries.

I value integrity as the most important guiding principle – for myself and others – but we're currently going through a crisis of integrity. There are increasing numbers of people who will do almost anything for financial reward, status symbols or online attention to garner likes, followers or clicks. It's vital that we have more integrity in what we do and reassess our values if we're going to meaningfully contribute to solving some of the world's problems and have fulfilling lives.

Here's one more personal example of mine that I'd like to share: I value longevity. I'm specifically referring to longevity of health-span, or, in other words, living as long a life as possible in a healthy state. That's what the poet Henry

David Thoreau was referring to when he said we need 'to live deep and suck out all the marrow of life' (Thoreau, 1854). Longevity isn't about defying aging, but maintaining good health for as long as possible. This strongly held value informs many of the decisions I make and the boundaries I set: 'Is this behaviour/habit/decision borrowing from tomorrow's health or happiness?' If the answer is yes, I reconsider that action.

Are there any habits or actions you're taking that might be borrowing from tomorrow? Skipping workouts, perhaps? Eating fast food or downgrading sleep in favour of staying up late? You might not be paying the consequences now, but will you be happy to pay that debt in the future?

The values you hold matter, especially when it comes to your resilience. Clearly defined personal values help you set boundaries, and boundaries influence your decisions, which affects the outcomes you get. In short, values build boundaries.

The paradox of values and boundaries

Resilience isn't about pushing through adversity (although I accept there will be times when you need to do that), but about knowing when *not* to, and that wisdom comes from being clear about your values. Values act as a filtration system. They protect energy, restore clarity and create the psychological safety needed to bounce forward, not just back.

Ask yourself

1. What principles are you unwilling to compromise, even when it's inconvenient or costly?
2. When have you felt proud of yourself, and what value (or values) were you honouring in that moment?
3. What situations make you feel frustrated or uncomfortable, and what does that reveal about your values?

SUSTAIN

4. If you could only be remembered for embodying three values, which would they be and why?
5. How do your daily actions and decisions reflect (or contradict) your core values?

TIP: NON-NEGOTIABLE VALUES CREATE UNBREAKABLE BOUNDARIES

Live today in a way your future self will thank you for. Ask yourself, is this habit borrowing from tomorrow's health or happiness? If yes, reconsider it. Let your personal values set the standard and your boundaries protect it. Long-term resilience starts with the choices you make now.

SIX

Identity Inspires Ownership

In the early days of running a business, I found myself in a tricky position with regard to sales and cashflow. Ultimately, the problem I was having was consistent sales revenue, but my more immediate problem was cashflow. Having spent a morning looking at the numbers, I came to the horrible realisation that we simply didn't have enough cash to cover all our outgoings at the end of the month. I'd pulled in every penny I could, but we were going to fall very

SUSTAIN

short of what we needed. My partner Antonia and I would have to jump off payroll straight away and take a three-month break from taking cash out of the business to rebuild. As you can imagine, this was a sobering time for us both.

I broke the news to Antonia who, after reeling from the shock, transferred some savings to cover herself. This left us with the question of how I would replace my salary. With meagre personal savings, I needed to find a job that I could walk straight into, and that ideally left me some time in the day to develop my business. I had the idea to contact a friend of mine who ran a local building company to see if they needed anyone. He told me that he needed another labourer, and I could start immediately. I'll be honest, I've never had any aspirations to work in the building trade, but this was an opportunity to start working immediately, and I would finish at 4pm, allowing me to keep working on my own business. I said yes and agreed to start the next day.

IDENTITY INSPIRES OWNERSHIP

Over the next few weeks, I turned up at different building sites at 8am sharp, wondering what the day would bring. I spent a lot of time in my discomfort zone, as I had absolutely no DIY or construction skills before this point. However, I remained open-minded and tried to be as adaptable as possible. Thanks to the generosity of the team, I learned a lot of skills, including plaster-boarding, repairing floorboards and ceilings, cutting out doorframes, bringing down walls with huge power tools, and even attempting some electrical wiring (under supervision, of course). I became familiar with power tools that initially scared me and was soon able to navigate a building site with a bit of confidence. At the time, I liked to joke that I learned enough to become dangerous at home since I'd have a go at DIY tasks that I wasn't entirely qualified to do! Throughout this time, though, I didn't lose sight of my true identity: that of a business owner. I was grateful to have work, but at no time did I think this was my new identity or that I was powerless over my situation. I remained focused on rebuilding the business as soon as I got back from the building sites.

Adapt and stay in the game

A few weeks into my labouring job, I received an email from someone who wanted to book me for a specific piece of work. I followed up on the opportunity, and eventually, an online meeting was set up so I could meet the CEO of the company. I took a hairbrush and a smart jumper to the building site, made sure I didn't take on any messy tasks that morning, and when the time for the call came, I brushed my hair, changed into my jumper and went out to my car to join the meeting. The call went well and after a couple of weeks of negotiations, we all signed up to a lucrative contract that meant I could leave the building site and get back to my previous role. I couldn't believe I'd been able to turn things around and was excited to get back

IDENTITY INSPIRES OWNERSHIP

to my old job, but this experience reinforced a powerful lesson: when we take ownership of our identity, we make choices that align with our long-term vision, even in tough times. I never abandoned my core identity, I adapted, but I never stopped being who I was. That's what made the difference. Resilience isn't just about surviving hard times; it's about holding onto our sense of identity so that we emerge stronger. The habits and choices we make every day either reinforce or weaken that identity; the key is to act in alignment with the person we want to become. I could have seen myself as a failure for not anticipating or planning for the cashflow crisis or felt defeated by circumstances. Instead, I reaffirmed my identity as a business owner, a problem solver, and someone who took ownership of my challenges.

Identity isn't about labels

Labels are descriptors which can be assigned to you by someone else, and they are often unhelpful or self-limiting. Labels can be unfounded and based on stereotypes, and they can damage our sense of self and general wellbeing if we start seeing ourselves through the judgements and biases of others. As opposed to labels, which are often derived from others, identifiers come from our own understanding of ourselves and the world around us. In other words, identity is self-defined. To cultivate a positive identity, we can focus on self-awareness, self-acceptance and building meaningful relationships. Identity is shaped when we explore our values, interests and strengths, and embrace our unique qualities.

The paradox of identity and behaviour

We think behaviour drives identity, but it's often identity that unlocks sustainable behaviour. In other words, who you believe you are shapes what you consistently do, even though that can feel counterintuitive if your actions don't always align with a world obsessed with high performance. When identity aligns with values (eg, 'I'm someone who protects my energy' or 'I'm a leader who prioritises wellbeing'), it becomes easier to take ownership of behaviours that *preserve* you, not deplete you.

SUSTAIN

Ask yourself

1. Who are you when things get difficult? Do you step up, withdraw, blame others or take control?

2. What are three words you would want others to use to describe you? Do your daily actions reflect that?

3. When have you felt most in your element? What were you doing? What strengths were you using?

4. What kind of person do you want to be five years from now, and what would that person do differently today?

5. When have you felt most like yourself? Look for patterns. Your values are hiding in plain sight.

TIP: RESPONDING TO CHALLENGES

Recall a time when you faced adversity. Did you see yourself as a victim of circumstance or an active problem solver? How would you have responded differently if you had been clearer about your identity?

SEVEN

Community Creates Connection

In 2023, Antonia and I took part in a three-day multiactivity event in the Arctic Circle. The first day was fat biking, the second day was cross-country skiing and the third and final day was snowshoeing. The terrain is testing but the scenery is breathtakingly beautiful. The event finishes at an iconic spot called the Three Country Cairn, which you can jog around in about twenty seconds and in doing so cross the borders of Finland, Norway and Sweden. On the morning of the first day, we woke to find natural light streaming through the gaps in the curtains. I got up to draw the curtains to reveal a snowscape, with only the mountains on the horizon. After a traditional Finnish breakfast, we set off for day one of the event, on the fat bikes we'd tested out the previous day. Within 500 metres we quickly realised that cycling through snow is every bit as hard as you'd imagine. We barely managed three revolutions of the pedals before falling off.

We had 40 kilometres to cover that day, and it was starting to look as though it would be a long one. After several aborted attempts to stay on the bikes, we gave up and pushed them through the snow. As we did so, we fell into step with another couple, Chris and Liz, and we started chatting. Even though we hadn't met them before, the conversation took our minds off the distance we had to cover and we eventually arrived at the checkpoint, about halfway into day one. It was at this point we realised that, somewhere along the way, we'd lost track of Liz. A little disconcerted about this, Chris decided to stay behind and wait for her, and Antonia and I carried on to the little hut to warm our hands and eat some food. We left the hut in low spirits, somewhat daunted by the prospect of pushing our bikes though yet more snow. We trudged along, resigning ourselves to hours of toil, when we heard a shout from behind us. Turning, we saw Chris running towards us; he realised that Liz must have gone ahead rather than fallen behind and was keen to get to the finish line to meet her. Having Chris join us lifted both our spirits. We were glad to see him, and he was pleased to have company. Everyone's mood improved and we all felt motivated to get to the finish line together – where, I'm pleased to say, Liz was waiting for us! Together we were stronger, and being in the company of like-minded people was also a real boost to our energy, mood and motivation. It only reinforces my belief that resilience is a lot to do with finding your tribe.

Social connection improves stress resilience

I love this quote from author and Happiness Researcher Shawn Achor:

> 'If you go through stress with the right lens and with other people, you can create meaningful narratives and social bonds that people will talk about for the rest of their lives.' (Achor, 2011)

Asking for the support of another person, whether that's mental, emotional or physical support, can often enable you to get a project over the line, a difficult decision made or complete a race or physical challenge. The science backs this up, too.

A study led by Simone Schnall at the University of Plymouth found that participants accompanied by a friend estimated a hill to be less steep when compared to participants who were alone

(Schall et al, 2008). Another study, led by Adam Doerrfeld, found that participants intending to lift a box with another person perceived it to be lighter than participants intending to lift the same box alone (provided that the other person appeared capable of helping) (Doerrfeld et al, 2011). Holding hands can also improve someone's perception of pain.

Can you think of a time that you were able to support another person, or they supported you? We are hard-wired to be tribal creatures. Resilience isn't about what you know, it's about who you are and what you care about.

The Blue Zones

The Blue Zones are five disparate parts of the world where an unusually large number of people live beyond eighty but in a good state of health (Blue Zones, 2025). (Fun fact, they are called the Blue Zones because the researchers used a blue pen to mark them on a map.) The regions include Loma Linda in California, Nicoya in Costa Rica, Sardinia in Italy, Icaria in Greece and Okinawa in Japan, and they were discovered by a group of researchers led by Belgian demographer Michel Poulain and Dan Buettner, who featured in the Netflix series of the same name. The team spent months studying the habits and lifestyles of the long-lived people in each region and came up with a set of characteristics they called the Power Nine. Three are particularly relevant to the theme of community and connection, illustrating that social connections and community are vital for longevity and therefore for personal sustainability:

- A sense of belonging
- Putting family first
- The feeling of being in the right tribe

The other elements related to nutrition and movement, but the overwhelming evidence suggests that social connection is a very real indicator of life expectancy. Isn't that interesting?

Seeking new connections

When we're looking to enhance social relationships or build a community, here's a little tip for you: start by looking at what's in front of you or in your immediate social network. In 2017, I was asked to take on a 'godparent-like' role to two young children, Rourke and Raven. (You might have noticed this book is dedicated to them.) I accepted, saying all the right things, but, if I'm honest, I didn't really do much. A year or so later, I realised that this was not only a great honour, but also a wonderful opportunity to be a role model to two young people and to build a meaningful relationship with them. I began seeing them every week and being fully present in the time we spent together. Fast forward to today and I have a great relationship with them, and it's very meaningful for me. Our

SUSTAIN

relationship will only grow and develop as they get older. My point, then, is simply that I had an untapped opportunity right there ready for me to see. What meaningful relationships or connections are right there under your nose, ready to be reestablished or engaged with?

COMMUNITY CREATES CONNECTION

The paradox of community and connection

Resilience is often framed as an individual trait, but often the stronger your support system is, the less you need to be strong all the time. We romanticise the lone wolf, but real resilience comes from pack behaviour. It's knowing who you can lean on, learn from, or laugh with when the pressure is on.

Ask yourself

1. When was the last time you felt truly connected to another person, and what impact did it have on your energy or mood that day?

2. Are you prioritising connections with others as much as you do your sleep, exercise or nutrition? If not, why not?

3. How might your environment (workplace, technology or culture) be subtly

SUSTAIN

   discouraging connection, even when you crave it?

4. What would it look like to build 'connection KPIs' into your daily life? For example, one meaningful conversation, one moment of shared laughter, one act of kindness.

5. Are you part of a tribe that reflects your values and supports your growth?

TIP: MEASURING CONNECTION

Connection is vital for wellbeing and resilience, but in a world obsessed with data and performance metrics, it can be hard to quantify. What if you measured wellbeing not just in sleep hours or workouts per week, but in *meaningful human interactions per day*?

EIGHT
Resources Support Resilience

In September 2019, my oldest friend and I embarked on an adventure in the Highlands of Scotland. We'd signed up for the Bear Grylls 'Survive the Highlands' flagship course, which is a five-day adventure during which you must survive on a ration pack; sleep out under the stars in shelters made from branches, moss and leaves; and learn Bear's survival skills, including rappelling, river crossing, night navigation, water purification, rope and knife skills, and foraging skills (interestingly named 'the edibles/dead-ibles game'). From the moment you arrive on site you are an hour away from a mobile signal, and you won't enter through a doorway or be under a roof for the next five days and four nights. Food is scarce as the entire point of the week is to test your resilience and ability to endure in as close to a real survival situation as possible.

The first morning starts early with physical training at 6am. Within minutes, Adam and I, along with the rest of the group, are crawling through a stream and are soaked from head to foot. Once that's done, we heat up a freeze-dried breakfast before setting out into the hills. It's Monday, and we won't return to camp until Friday morning. By Thursday, we're all tired, hungry, cold and keen to have a hot shower and a warm bed, but the instructors have something else in mind – a twenty-four-hour simulated self-rescue. The purpose of this exercise is to apply the skills we've learned over the last few days to a scenario designed to replicate an actual survival situation.

We're given the coordinates for a site in a woodland and a radio, and we're told to message the instructors when we find it. We do so, and are told to make camp for the night, then radio again at 0600 hours with the coordinates of the highest peak visible to us from camp. After a very wet and restless night, we radio through the coordinates of various peaks until we get the right one. We are then instructed to pack up camp, leaving no trace, and make our way within forty minutes, as a single group, to the peak, where we will meet a rescue team (not an actual rescue, obviously) that will take us back down the mountain to safety. Everything is a blur at this point as we must move fast, and no one is feeling energetic. Climbing the mountain at pace causes a lot of issues as fitness levels differ, as does motivation. Once at the top, the instructor, Martin, gives us all a piece of chocolate, before instructing us to follow

SUSTAIN

him as he jogs down the mountain. We have no choice but to follow, as he's moving with the same level of urgency as there would be in an actual rescue situation. We aren't following paths but jogging through bracken and heather; every step is a leap of faith, but, amazingly, no one is injured. At the bottom of the mountain, we're given harnesses, clipped onto a cable and told to start crossing a ravine using a technique we've learned called a Tyrolean rope crossing. At the other side, we're rushed along a track before arriving at the Land Rover. The experience is over, the events of the last hour a blur to us all. We arrive at the lodge in a catatonic state and, removing our helmets and harnesses, we shower and consume copious amounts of cooked food.

What I learned from this experience is the importance of having resources that support resilience. Resources can be physical objects, like fitness equipment, but they can also be ideas, habits and mantras. Learning about survival

RESOURCES SUPPORT RESILIENCE

tactics taught me that, when your resilience is challenged and you're feeling overwhelmed, there is a beautiful simplicity in stopping. You can take some of the realisations I had during this experience:

- You may not be overwhelmed by a PT exercise first thing in the morning, but you might be deluged with emails or tasks in any given day.
- You may not have to navigate by the stars, but you might be struggling to navigate the internal politics of your organisation or navigate your way through peak rush hour.
- You might not be racing up a mountain in a simulated self-rescue scenario, but instead rushing from the school run to your first meeting and then chasing your tail for the rest of the day.

Poor decisions are made when we rush. Stop, gather your thoughts, and then break down what's ahead of you into small, manageable chunks – the next task, the next hour, the next call. Another crucial lesson is not to think too far ahead; be present for each chunk of time or task. One way of thinking about this is what I call the Minimal Effective Day.

The Minimal Effective Day

The Minimal Effective Day is a strategy that involves stripping your day down to the essentials, focusing only on the tasks that truly need to be done to move you closer to your objectives. What's the minimum you can do today that will still have a positive impact? You're not cutting corners on what's critical, but you're eliminating the noise, the tasks that don't need to be done today, don't need to be done by you, or maybe that don't need to be done at all. By doing this, you can free up resources to focus on what matters. All our energy comes from the same place, meaning we don't have a reservoir of energy for work, another for socialising and another for working out. We only have so much on any given day, and we need to ensure it's used wisely and that we replenish it. It's about maintaining our energy, mood and motivation, ensuring we have the resilience to thrive. Like I say, everything lies downstream of energy, mood and motivation.

Rocks and pebbles

One of my personal mantras is 'Small changes, big impact'. We often overestimate what we can achieve in a short period of time but underestimate the power of small changes over time. It's also a lot easier to introduce small habits that build into some big changes – I call this idea 'rocks and pebbles', and it's helpful when we think about the personal resources that we have to support our resilience.

'Rocks' might be things like hiring a personal trainer or joining a gym, making significant changes to your diet (for example, becoming vegetarian or going sugar-free), changing your sleep routine or giving up caffeine. Rocks are the big stuff. They're noble ambitions but they're not always easy to achieve or make habitual.

'Pebbles' are small actions that can still be very significant. For example, standing up to take phone calls to encourage more movement, putting an electrolyte tablet into your water to boost hydration, ordering an extra side of vegetables with dinner to add more nutrients or buying an eye mask to improve the quality of your sleep. It's much easier to build these small habits into your life, and their overall impact is often greater than the sum of their parts – more movement results in greater blood flow and muscle tone, there is evidence to show that every portion of fruit and vegetables eaten helps protect us against heart disease and strokes by up to 30% and some cancers by up to 20% (BDA,

2023), and getting adequate sleep can result in a 60% improvement in the glymphatic system (Pollard, 2019). Small changes, big impact.

The paradox of resources and resilience

Real resilience isn't built during moments of crisis but developed in the moments of calm. The paradox is that most people only think

SUSTAIN

about resilience when they're already under pressure. By then, you're in firefighting mode. In fact, resilience is built by the quiet work. It's in the routines you stick to, the sleep you prioritise, the boundaries you protect and the people you lean on. That's the real paradox: if you're getting resilience right, it won't look like you need it.

Ask yourself

1. When you're under pressure, can you find moments to stop or slow down to prioritise recovery?
2. What are the pebbles you can prioritise daily to replenish your energy?
3. What's your Minimal Effective Day, and are you honest about what truly needs to be done?
4. When you're feeling drained and everything seems to be an uphill slog,

what inner strength or belief helps you take the next step?

5. Are you building habits today that will hold steady when life gets unpredictable, or are you waiting for something to happen to force a change?

TIP: AGENCY IS THE ENGINE OF RESILIENCE

When you believe you have choice and influence, you're more likely to act, adapt and recover. Even in difficult situations, reclaiming small moments of control – how you respond, what you focus on, where you put your energy – builds strength.

A Final Message: The Ultimate Paradox

Allow me to take you back to the Arctic Circle event that I described to you in Chapter Six. The night before the event, the lead guide, Rob, gathered us together for a briefing. He went through the safety details, talked through the mandatory kit list and shared a few other important details. Just as we thought he was finished, Rob paused, before startling us with his most important piece of advice: 'Be arsed'.

> 'There will be times when you're out there on the bike, and you'll know you need to cover your face with the buff,

SUSTAIN

> but you'll think to yourself, "I can't be arsed to stop." There will be times when you feel the beginnings of a small blister appear on your heel, but you'll think, "I can't be arsed to put a plaster on." There will be times when you feel thirsty, but you can't be arsed to stop for a drink or think, "I'll stop later." Be arsed.'

Rob strongly encouraged us to be arsed, as it's the little things that add up to much bigger things and can have a significant impact on overall performance. It was such an unexpected phrase that it really got our attention, and if I'm honest, it's disarmingly accurate because that's often exactly what's going on in our heads. We intuitively know we should stand up for a bit, stretch our backs, get a glass of water or head out for a healthy bite to eat, but sometimes we choose to stay at our desks or (subconsciously) think, 'I can't be arsed'. The reality is that these minor choices directly impact our energy, mood

A FINAL MESSAGE: THE ULTIMATE PARADOX

and motivation. They affect our resilience. The things we *can't be arsed* to do in the moment are often the very things that sustain us in the long run.

In the context of an endurance event, Rob knew that a small thing like a blister can literally stop you in your tracks. Small actions add up – positively and negatively. Taking care of yourself in the moment makes the difference between thriving and struggling, whether you're in the Arctic or sitting at your desk.

SUSTAIN

Perhaps the ultimate paradox is that most of us know what we need to do to sustain our energy, mood and motivation, but find ourselves thinking 'I can't be arsed', or something else takes priority. Next time you find yourself delaying or deliberating, keep this important mantra in your head: Be arsed!

Bibliography

Achor, S (2011) 'The happy secret to better work' (TEDxBloomington), www.ted.com/talks/shawn_achor_the_happy_secret_to_better_work, accessed 26 May 2025

Blue Zones (2025) 'Blue Zones: We empower everyone, everywhere to live better, longer', www.bluezones.com, accessed 26 May 2025

British Dietetic Association (2023) 'Fruit and vegetables: How to get 5 a day', www.bda.uk.com/resource/fruit-and-vegetables-how-to-get-five-a-day.html, accessed 26 May 2025

Ciphr (2024) 'Workplace stress statistics in the UK in 2024', www.ciphr.com/infographics/workplace-stress-statistics, accessed 5 June 2025

Creswell, JD, Welch, WT, Taylor, SE, Sherman, DK, Gruenewald, TL and Mann, T (2005) 'Affirmation of personal values buffers neuroendocrine and psychological stress responses', *Psychological Science*, 16(11), 846–851, https://doi.org/10.1111/j.1467-9280.2005.01624.x, accessed 7 July 2025

Doerrfeld, A, Sebanz, N and Shiffrar, M (2011) 'Expecting to lift a box together makes the load look lighter', *Psychological Research*, 76/4, pp467–75, https://pmc.ncbi.nlm.nih.gov/articles/PMC3383959, accessed 26 May 2025

Mental Health UK (2025) 'Burnout Report 2025 reveals generational divide in levels of stress and work absence', https://mentalhealth-uk.org/blog/burnout-report-2025-reveals-generational-divide-in-levels-of

-stress-and-work-absence, accessed 26 May 2025

Merani, M (2023) 'According to OpenAI CEO Sam Altman, this is the skill that entrepreneurs must absolutely have to ensure their success', *Middle East Entrepreneur*, www.entrepreneur.com/en-ae/news-and-trends/according-to-openai-ceo-sam-altman-heres-the-skill-that/453786, accessed 26 May 2025

Moss, R (2024) 'Employers face a "soft skills crisis"', *Personnel Today*, www.personneltoday.com/hr/employers-face-a-soft-skills-crisis, accessed 26 May 2025

Pollard, H (2019) 'Disrupted sleep: A cause or consequence of Alzheimer's?' (Alzheimer's Research UK), www.alzheimersresearchuk.org/news/disrupted-sleep-a-cause-or-consequence-of-alzheimers, accessed 26 May 2025

Rosling, H, with O Rosling and AR Rönnlund (2018) *Factfulness: Ten reasons we're wrong about the world – and why things are better than you think* (Sceptre)

Schnall, S, Harber, KD, Stefanucci, JK and Proffitt, DR (2008) 'Social support and the perception of geographical slant', *Journal of Experimental Social Psychology*, 1/44(5), pp1246–1255, https://pmc.ncbi.nlm.nih.gov/articles/PMC3291107, accessed 26 May 2025

Sheldon, KM and Elliot, AJ (1999) 'Goal striving, need satisfaction, and longitudinal wellbeing: The self-concordance model', *Journal of Personality and Social Psychology*, 76(3), pp482–497, https://doi.org/10.1037/0022-3514.76.3.482, accessed 5 June 2025

Spencer, L (2016) 'Why fitness is more important than weight' (TEDx Wandsworth), TEDx talk, www.youtube.com/watch?v=-SLP1BF7KBQ, accessed 21 May 2025

Spencer, L (2025) *The State of Workplace Wellbeing* (Leanne Spencer), https://leannespencer.co.uk/resources/state-of

-workplace-wellbeing-report, accessed 5 June 2025

Thoreau, HD (1854) *Walden*: Or, *Life in the Woods* (Ticknor and Fields)

Bonus Resources

The 12 Stages of Burnout

https://leannespencer.co.uk/the-12-stages-of-burnout

A guide to recognising the signs of burnout, with tips for recovery and supporting others.

The State of Workplace Wellbeing Report 2025

https://leannespencer.co.uk/resources/state-of-workplace-wellbeing-report

A deep dive into the connection between employee wellbeing and an organisation's success.

The Cadence Wellbeing Scorecard

https://leannespencer.co.uk/cadence-scorecard

A tool to help you monitor your work–life balance and manage your wellbeing.

Leanne Spencer's Blog Archive

https://leannespencer.co.uk/blog

Here you can find all my blogs on resilience, wellbeing, the Sustain framework and more.

Be Arsed: Personal sustainability principles

https://leannespencer.co.uk/sustain-framework

The Sustain Framework questions help you create your own personal sustainability principles.

BONUS RESOURCES

Cadence: The secret to beating burnout and performing in life and work

https://leannespencer.co.uk/cadence-book

This book teaches you how to apply a simple and effective approach to your life. It's the secret to beating burnout and performing in life and work.

Rise and Shine: Recover from burnout and get back to your best

www.amazon.co.uk/Rise-Shine-Recover
-burnout-back/dp/1781333734

In this book, I share my expertise and experience to show you how to spot the signs of professional burnout, recover and go on to enjoy a happier, healthier life and career.

The Author

Leanne Spencer is an award-winning speaker and author. With over thirteen years in the wellbeing sector, thirteen qualifications in exercise and nutrition, and more than 1000 presentations delivered, Leanne is a leading voice on integrating wellbeing into high-performance cultures. She has delivered a TEDx talk with over 132,000 views, authored three bestselling books including *Cadence*, a finalist in the

Business Book Awards, and has been Highly Commended at the London Speaker Awards.

Through her signature keynotes – Cadence, BOND and Sustain – Leanne shows audiences how to achieve sustainable performance by managing energy, strengthening connections and building personal resilience. Clients include Britvic, Vax, JP Morgan, Nestlé, Amazon, England Netball, BUNZL, Asana, Engie, Outward Bound Trust, Circle Health, Belron International and many more, including charities, the NHS and public sector organisations.

Sustain is Leanne's fourth book, after the bestselling books *Rise and Shine*, *Remove the Guesswork* and *Cadence*. Leanne loves watching sport, playing golf, fitness, reading, hiking and spending time with her partner Antonia, their two cats and Kami, their Romanian rescue dog. Leanne and her family split their time between London and Margate.

THE AUTHOR

You can follow Leanne on social media or visit her website for videos and blogs:

- www.leannespencer.co.uk
- www.facebook.com/leannespencerkeynote
- www.linkedin.com/in/leannespencerkeynote
- @leannespencerkeynote